GERMAN HEADGEAR IN WORLD WAR II

German Headgear in World War II

Vol.II: SS/NSDAP/POLICE/CIVILIAN/MISC.

A Photographic Study of German Hats and Helmets

Pat Moran & Jon A. Maguire

Schiffer Military History
Atglen, PA

Book Design by Robert Biondi.

Library of Congress Catalog Number: 96-70420.

Printed in Hong Kong.
ISBN: 0-7643-0245-0

We are interested in hearing from authors with book ideas on related topics.

Published by Schiffer Publishing Ltd.
4880 Lower Valley Road
Atglen, PA 19310
Phone: (610) 593-1777
FAX: (610) 593-2002
E-mail: Schifferbk@aol.com.
Please write for a free catalog.
This book may be purchased from the publisher.
Please include $2.95 postage.
Try your bookstore first.

Introduction

Headgear of the Third Reich period has been studied and collected virtually from the time of its introduction. The shear number of variations coupled with the quality and beauty of tailoring, has created a large interest in this subject. Throughout history, the Germans have been known for their strikingly beautiful military uniforms. In the Wehrmacht of World War II, each branch of service wore a unique, identifying color of trim, or piping (waffenfarbe), on the cap and uniform coat. As a result, a beautiful collection can be assembled of caps from just the Army or Luftwaffe alone! Not only did the German military forces have tremendous variations of uniforms, many professionals such as the police, railway workers, postal workers, diplomats, political leaders, forestry officials, firefighters, etc., also wore military style uniforms!

In these two volumes, we have tried to assemble as many authentic examples of Third Reich headgear as possible, without being redundant. It is intended to serve as a photographic reference for collectors and historians, and is in no way intended to glorify this dark period in German history. The regulations and history of this headgear has been written numerous times in many fine books. We hope this work will add to that collective knowledge.

A project of this magnitude would not be possible without the help of many individuals. Our thanks goes out to the following people: Bob Biondi, Peter Schiffer, Dave Webster, Harper Noehren, Arthur Hayes, Jack Hatter, Bill Rentz, Bill Shea, Dale Edwards, Tim Smetana, John Johnson, Bob Sevier, Mike Davidson, Mike Whitson, Matthew Reinert, Irv Marine, Bill Dienna, Rob Rumbold, and Mike Conner. Special thanks to Linda and Toby Moran for letting us destroy their dining room for a week, so we could shoot photographs!

Every effort has been made to accurately reproduce the colors of the hats in this book. However, due to age, variations of dye lots, fabric materials, and technicalities of lighting and ink lots there may be some variations to the actual shades.

4

SS

Allgemeine-SS General Officer's Visor Cap

Cap is made of a high quality black doeskin wool material with a black velvet cap band. Cap also has a silver national emblem and SS-Totenkopf (death's head) and is piped in silver wire with aluminum chincord. *(Hayes)*

Allgemeine-SS Officer's Visor Cap

Cap is made of black doeskin wool with a black velvet cap band. Cap has a silver national emblem and SS-Totenkopf and is piped in white (weiss) waffenfarbe with aluminum chincord. *(Hayes)*

56

Early Allgemeine-SS Enlisted Visor Cap

Cap is made of black wool with a black cap band and has the early pattern national emblem and Hussar style jawless Totenkopf. Cap has a black leather chin strap. *(Hayes)*

Gruppe West
Wasserdicht
Stirndruckfrei
D.R.P.

Allgemeine-SS Enlisted Visor Cap

Cap has black leather chin strap and white (weiss) waffenfarbe. *(Hayes)*

Early Allgemeine-SS Feldmütze

This cap was styled after the Imperial period Feldmütze and is dated 1933. *(Hayes)*

Late Pattern Allgemeine-SS Feldmütze

(Hayes)

Allgemeine-SS Double Decal M18 Helmet with Black Satin Finish

(Hayes)

Waffen-SS Officer's Visor Cap

This cap is made of high quality field grey wool, with black velvet cap band, piped in white (weiss) waffenfarbe. National emblem and SS-Totenkopf are metal. *(Hayes)*

Waffen-SS Officer's Visor Cap

A second example. Cap has metal insignia and white (weiss) waffenfarbe. *(Hayes)*

59

Waffen-SS Officer's Visor Cap

A third example. Cap has metal insignia and white (weiss) waffenfarbe. Note private makers label. *(Edwards)*

Waffen-SS NCO's "Old Style" Visor Cap

Cap is made of a field grey wool material with black cap band and piped in white (weiss) waffenfarbe. Cap has metal national emblem and SS death's head. Note that the cloth visor is the same color as the crown. *(Noebren)*

Waffen-SS NCO/EM Visor Cap

Cap is made of a filed grey wool material with black wool cap band and piped in white (weiss) waffenfarbe. Cap has metal national emblem and SS death's head with black leather chin strap. *(Noebren)*

SS-VT M38 Feldmütze

Note white soutache, and Totenkopf button on the front. *(Hayes)*

Waffen-SS M35 Double Decal Helmet

Waffen-SS Tropical Pith Helmet

Helmet has SS runes on the right side, and party color shield on the left side. *(Hayes)*

Waffen-SS Green Fez

Early green fez of the 13th Waffen-SS Handschar Division. Fez has bevo machine-woven insignia and was worn with the battle dress uniform. *(Reinert)*

Waffen-SS Red Fez

Red fez with bevo machine-woven insignia. Fez was worn with the parade or walking-out uniform. *(Reinert)*

5

POLICE

Police General's Visor Cap

Cap is made of a green-mottled doeskin material with a dark brown cap band and gilt metal second pattern (1936-45) two piece Police eagle with gilt nylon piping and cords. Cap was manufactured by EREL.

Municipal Police Officer's Visor Cap

Cap has a dark brown band and wine red (weinrot) waffenfarbe with a two piece Police eagle. Cap was manufactured by EREL.

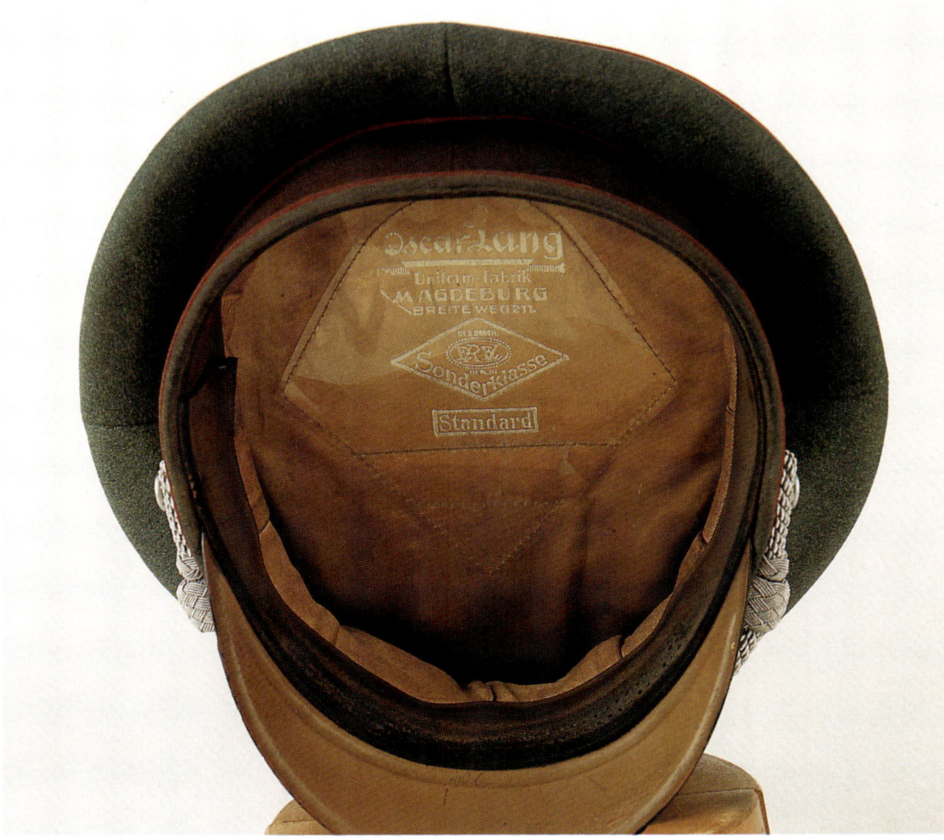
Oscar Lang
MAGDEBURG
Sonderklasse
Standard

Enlisted Municipal Policeman's Visor Cap

Cap has metal insignia and black leather chin strap.

National Police Officer's Visor Cap

Cap has a dark brown band and light green (hellgrun) waffenfarbe. Cap also has a high quality second pattern (1936-45) two piece Police eagle and was manufactured by EREL.

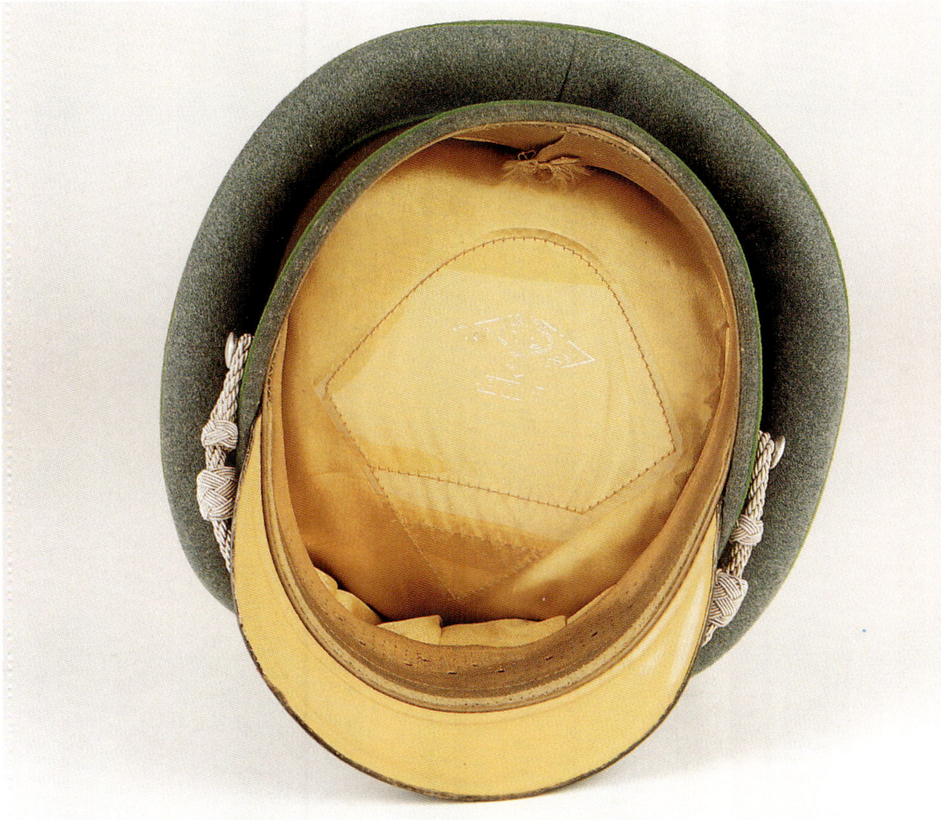

National Police Officer's White Summer Service Cap

Cap has dark brown band, and light green (hellgrun) waffenfarbe, with metal eagle and aluminum chin cord.

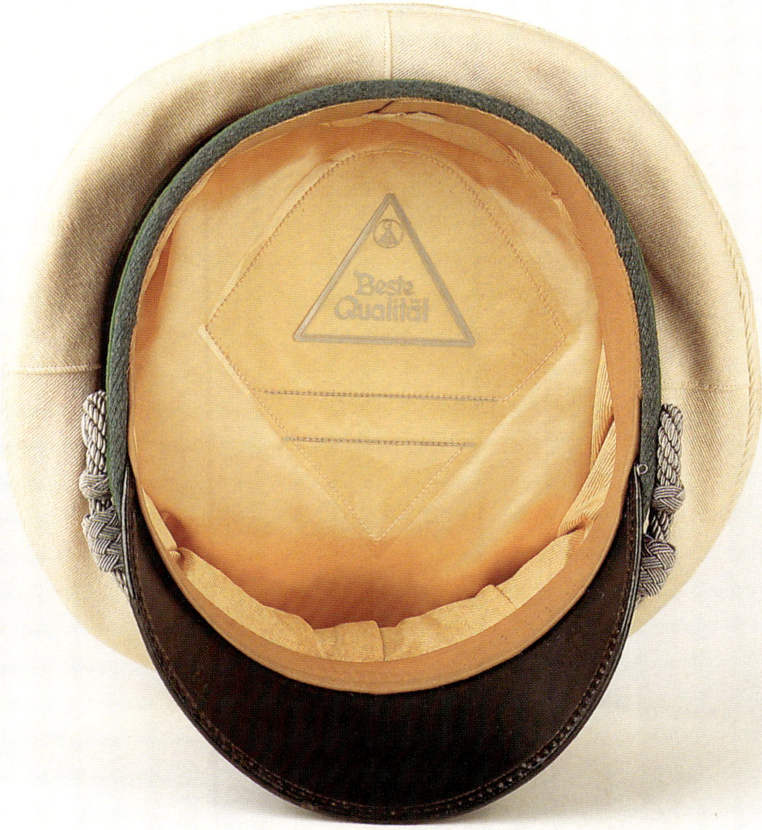
Beste
Qualität

Gendarmerie Officer's Visor Cap

Cap has a dark brown band with orange waffenfarbe. Cap was manufactured by Clemens Wagner and appears to be an NCO upgrade to officer. *(Rentz)*

BRAUNSCHWEIG
56 ½

Enlisted Gendarmerie Policeman's Visor Cap

Cap has metal insignia and black leather chin strap. *(Dienna)*

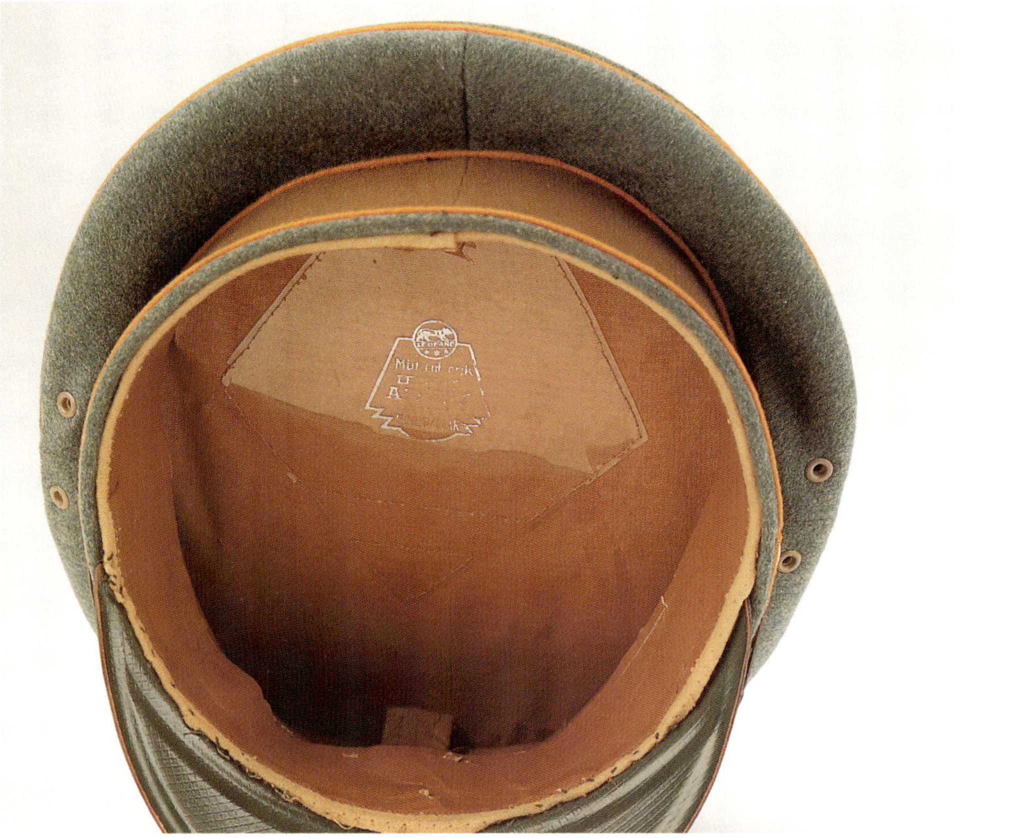

Administration Police Officer's Visor Cap

Cap has a high quality second pattern (1936-45) two piece Police eagle and light grey (hellgrau) waffenfarbe. *(Rentz)*

Autobahn Police (Motorisierten Gendarmeriebereitschaft) Enlisted Visor Cap

Cap has an olive mottled wool body with white cap band and white (weiss) waffenfarbe with a gold second pattern Police eagle and black leather chin strap with gold buttons. Cap was manufactured by Robert Lubstein. Note the screened air vents. *(Rentz)*

Robert Lubstein
Berlin N.W.21
Alt Moabit

Fire Protection Police (1939-1942) Officer's Visor Cap

Cap is made of a mottled green wool with a black cap band and carmine red (karmesinrot) waffenfarbe. Cap was manufactured by EREL. *(Rentz)*

Fire Police Officer's Visor Cap

Cap is made of a dark blue doeskin material with a black velvet cap band and carmine red (karmesinrot) waffenfarbe. Cap has the first pattern (1934-36) Police eagle and vented metal national cockade. Cap was manufactured by EREL. *(Rentz)*

Sonderklasse

Second Example - Fire Police Officer's Visor Cap

This cap was manufactured by Pekuro. Note the flecking in the chin cord. *(Shea)*

PREISGEKRÖNTE
Pekürо Mütze
Deutsches Reichs-Patent
Herm. Schellkorn
Offenbach

Police Officer's Parade Dress Shako

(Hayes)

Enlisted Traffic Policeman's Summer Shako

Shako is manufactured by EREL. *(Hayes)*

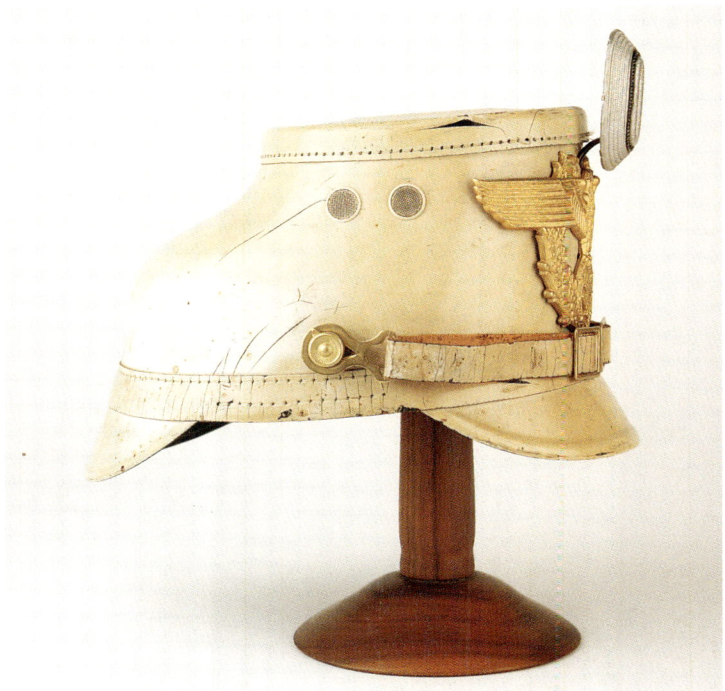

White Leather Traffic Control Police Crash Helmet

Helmet was manufactured by EREL. *(Hayes)*

M35 Double Decal Police Helmet

(Hayes)

M40 Double Decal Police Helmet

M34 Fire Police Double Decal Helmet

Helmet has leather neck flap. *(Hayes)*

6

NSDAP

Reichsleiter Political Leader's Visor Cap

Cap has a light brown wool top with a brown velvet cap band and yellow (gelbe) waffenfarbe. Cap has a gilt metal NSDAP insignia and gold nylon chincord.

Reichsleitung Political Leader's Visor Cap

Cap has a dark brown wool top with brown velvet band. The cap is marked to the Ordenburgen School (NSDAP Political Training Centers). Cap has yellow (gelbe) waffenfarbe.

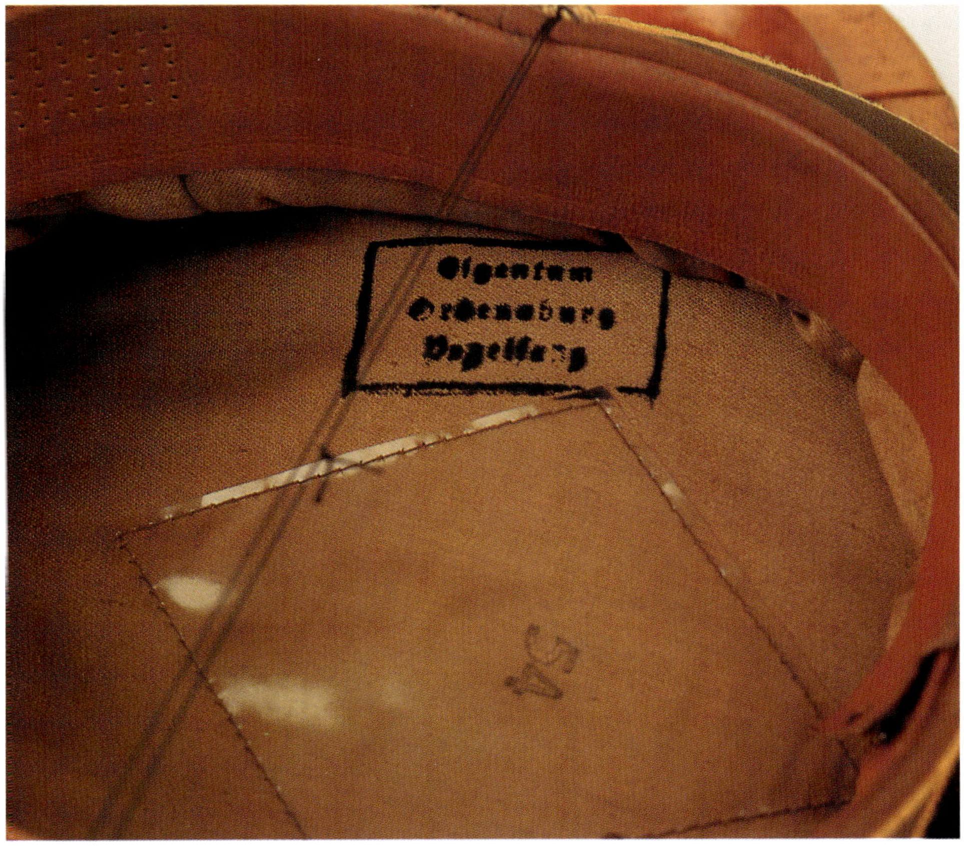
Eigentum
Ordensburg
Vogelsang

Reichsleitung Political Leader's White Topped Summer Visor Cap

Cap has a white high-quality wool top with a brown velvet cap band and yellow (gelbe) waffenfarbe. Cap also has gilt metal NSDAP insignia. *(Rentz)*

Unissued Gauleiter Political Leader's Visor Cap

Cap has red (rot) waffenfarbe. Note that the wreath is embroidered directly into the cap band. Also note the RZM tag on chin strap.

Unissued Gauleiter Political Leader's Visor Cap

Second example. *(Hayes)*

Kreisleiter Political Leader's Visor Cap

Cap has black (schwarz) waffenfarbe.

1939 Kreisleiter Political Leader's Visor Cap

The war years brought a change in the Kreisleiter waffenfarbe from black to white.

Ortsgruppenleiter Political Leader's Visor Cap

Cap has light blue (hellblau) waffenfarbe.

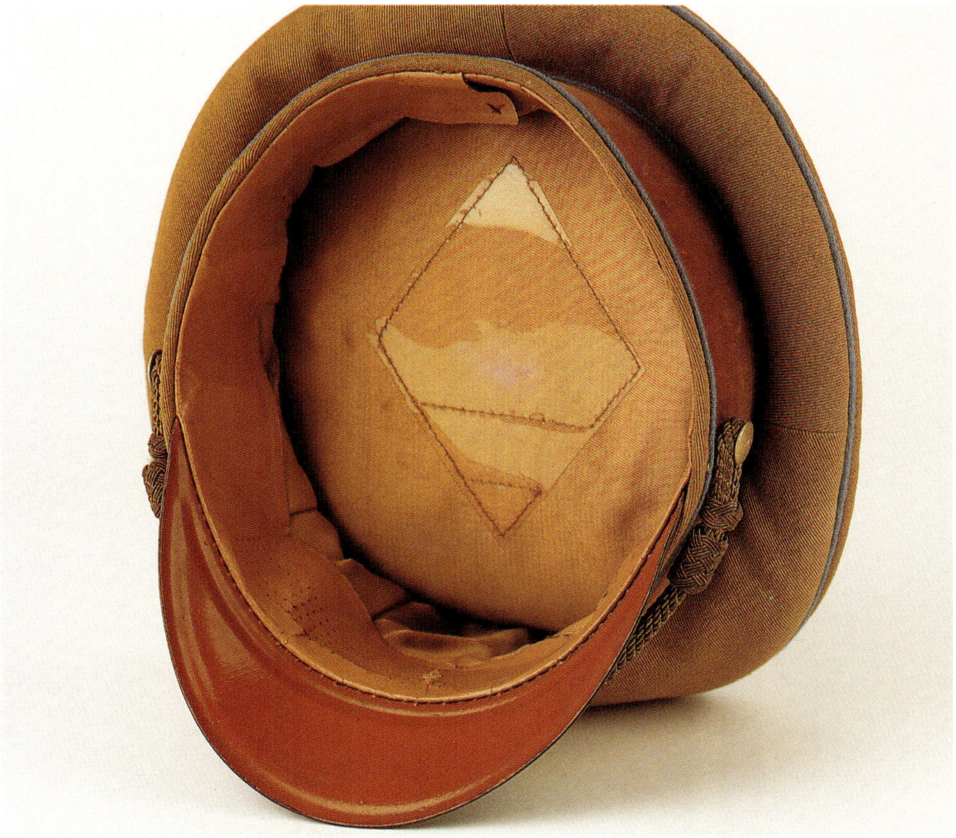

Ortsgruppenleiter Political Leader's Visor Cap

Second example. *(Hayes)*

Ortsgruppenleiter Political Leader's White Topped Summer Visor Cap

Cap has a white top with brown velvet cap band. Note this cap was made in Rome. *(Hayes)*

BERRETTIFICIO
PIEDIMONTE
ROMA

7

MISC.

Hitler Youth High Leader's Visor Cap

Cap is made of a light brown wool material with a black velvet cap band. Cap has a silver second pattern Party style eagle with gilt piping and cords and enameled HJ diamond. *(Rentz)*

Stirndruckfrei

Hitler Youth Leader Visor Cap

Cap is made of a light brown wool material with black velvet cap band. Cap has a silver metal Party style eagle, piping and cords with enameled HJ diamond and is named to a Ch. Keller, RJF, München. *(Hayes)*

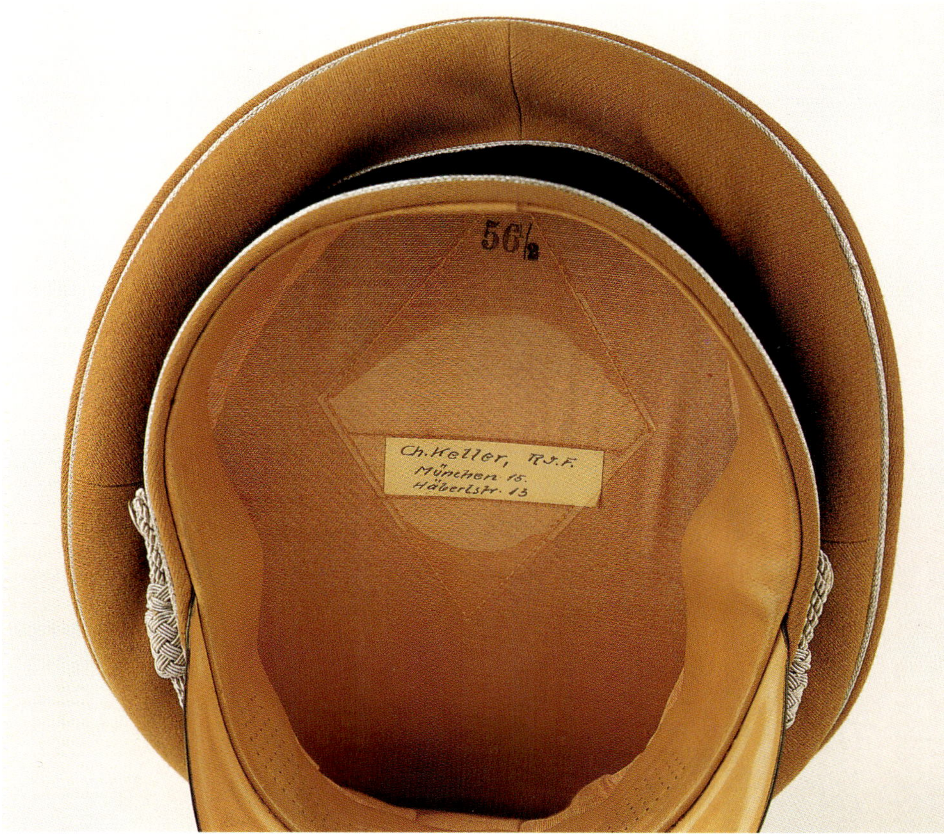
56½
Ch. Keller, RJF.
München 15.
Häberlstr. 13

Hitler Youth Leader's Visor Cap

Cap is made of a light brown wool material with silver metal Party style eagle, cap band piping and cords. Note the red (rot) crown waffenfarbe denoting the ranks of Gefolgschaftsführer to Oberstammführer. *(Rentz)*

NSKK (National Socialist Motor Corps) Officer's Visor Cap

Cap has a brown wool top with a dark brown cap band and waffenfarabe. Cap has a metal NSKK national emblem, cockade and aluminum chin cord. *(Hayes)*

Otto Zillmann
Mützenmacherei
Schweinfurt a. M.
Markt 22

German Red Cross (Deutsches Rotes Kreuz) Officer's Visor Cap

Cap has light grey wool top with a dark grey cap band and grey-white waffenfarbe. Cap has enameled Red Cross eagle, swastika and cross, and silvered metal cap wreath and is named to Wilh. Liehsener.

Second Example of German Red Cross Officer's Visor Cap

Cap has an aluminum chin cord. *(Rentz)*

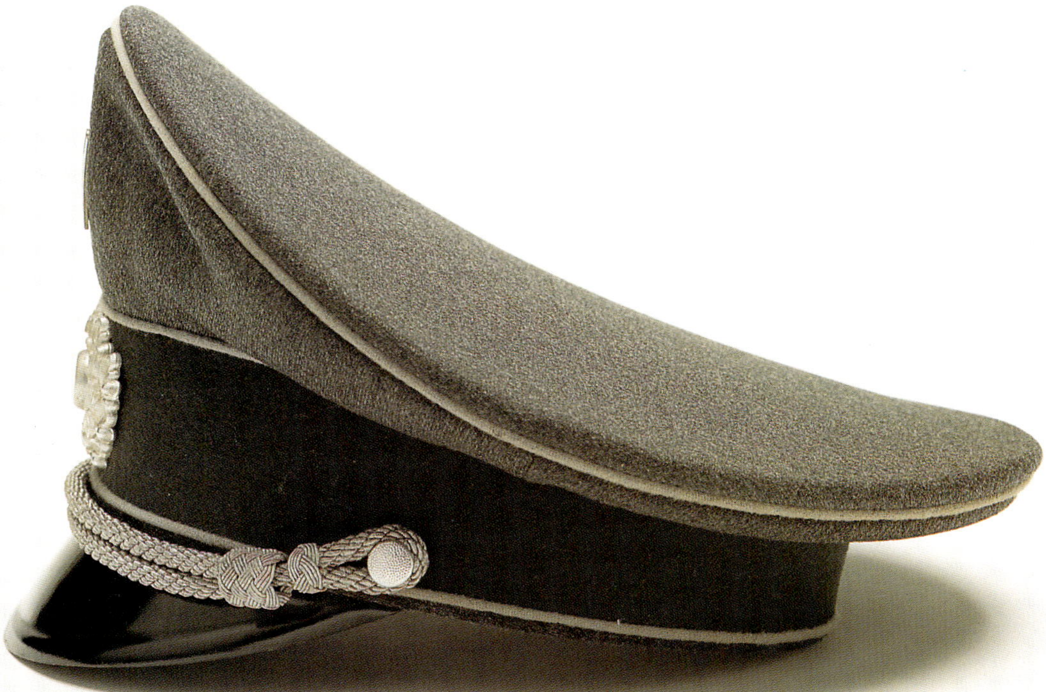

58

German Red Cross Enlisted Visor Cap

Cap has an enameled Red Cross eagle and metal cockade with black leather chin strap. *(Rentz)*

Heinrich Schmidt

German Customs Officer's Visor Cap

Cap has a field-grey wool top with medium green cap band and waffenfarbe. Cap has a distinctive metal customs eagle with its wing tips slightly turned up and a metal cockade with a silver cap cord with green flecking. *(Hayes)*

München 2

Second Example of German Customs Officer's Visor Cap.

Cap was manufactured by EREL. *(Rentz)*

WIEN IX.
Sonderklasse
Standard

Railway Police (Bahnpolizei) Officer's Visor Cap

Cap is made of a mottled blue-grey wool with black velvet cap band and silver piping. Cap has a silver metal eagle with bullion embroidered wreath and metal cockade. *(Rentz)*

BRAUNSCHWEIG

Railway Service (Reichsbahn) High Ranking Official's Visor Cap

Cap is made of a dark blue doeskin material with a black velvet cap band and bright red piping. Cap has a flat gilt second pattern Party style eagle with a gilt metal "flying wheel" wreath and a silver metal cockade. Note the gilt chincord. *(Hayes)*

Albert Ziegler
Giengen a. Brenz
Fil. Bachhagel

Railway Service (Reichsbahn) Middle Ranks Official's Visor Cap

Cap is made of a dark blue wool material with a black cap band and bright red piping. Note the gold and blue cap cord. *(Rentz)*

57
Peter Küpper
Wu.-Ronsdorf

National Forestry Officer's Visor Cap

This cap is made of grey-green wool fabric with dark green (dunkelgrun) waffenfarbe and cap band. Cap has silver metal Forestry eagle with wire embroidered wreath and metal cockade. *(Rentz)*

Diplomatic Official's Visor Cap

Cap is made of black doeskin material with silver wire piping, eagle, wreath, cockade and chincord. Cap was manufactured by EREL. *(Rentz)*

Sonderklasse
Privat

SA Marine Visor Cap

Cap is made of dark navy blue material with mohair cap band and gilt metal national emblem and wreath with SA insignia. Cap was made by A. Lang of Darmstadt. *(Rentz)*

Uniformmützen
u. Effekten
Ordensdekorationen
A. Lang
Darmstadt
Dieburgerstraße 62
früher Alexanderstr. u. Kaserne
gegr. 1882
Müller

D.A.F. (Deutsche Arbeitsfront) Visor Cap

Cap is made of high quality doeskin with oakleaves and acorns embroidered on the cap band. All national insignia is embroidered from silver wire. *(Rentz)*

Stirndruckfrei
Deutsches Reichspatent

D.A.F. NCO/EM Visor Cap

Cap is made of quality black wool fabric with oakleaves and acorns embroidered in the band. All insignia is metal and chin strap is black leather. *(Rentz)*

56

D.A.F. Festival Enlisted Visor Hat

Cap is made of black wool with woven cap band and insignia. Insignia is surrounded by a metal oval. Chin strap is leather. *(Rentz)*

Reichsluftschutzbund (RLB) Officer's Visor Cap

Cap is made of blue-grey wool with black cap band and silver piping. The eagle and wreath are bullion and the cockade is metal. Cap manufactured by EREL. *(Rentz)*

RLB NCO/Enlisted Visor Cap

Cap is made of blue-grey wool with black cap band and lilac waffenfarbe. The insignia is metal and chinstrap is leather. *(Rentz)*

Soldatenbund Visor Cap for Infantry

Cap is made of dark blue wool with black ribbed mohair band. Waffenfarbe is white (weiss) for a former infantryman. Insignia is metal and chin strap is leather. *(Rentz)*

Die vorschriftsmäßige Mütze
des Soldatenbundes
Bethmann

Soldatenbund Visor Cap for Cavalry

Waffenfarbe is golden yellow for a former cavalryman. *(Rumbold)*

Getes
Die vorschriftsmäßige Mütze
des Soldatenbundes
Ges. gesch.
56

Soldatenbund Visor Cap for Artillery

Red (rot) waffenfarbe denotes a veteran of the artillery. Note the Maltese cross in the center of the cockade. *(Rumbold)*

Die vorschriftsmäßige Mütze
des Soldatenbundes
Ges. gesch.

National Socialist Deutscher Marine-Bund Visor Cap

Cap is made of dark blue wool with black ribbed mohair band. Insignia is gilt metal. Chin strap is black leather. *(Dienna)*

TENO Officer's Visor Cap

National emblem and wreath are bullion wire and cockade is metal. EREL is the maker of this quality cap. *(Rentz)*

Ministry of the Occupied Eastern Territories Officer's Visor Cap

Cap is made of orange-brown wool with dark brown band. The eagle and wreath are bullion wire and the cockade is metal. *(Marine)*

Reichsmarshall Hermann Goring's Personal Visor Cap

This is one of several caps worn by the Reichsmarshall. This example was made by EREL. All bullion insignia is embroidered directly on the fabric of the cap. Note this example does not have the laurel leaf motif embroidered on the cap band which Goring sometimes wore. The visor is made of leather. *(Marine)*

Also from the Publisher

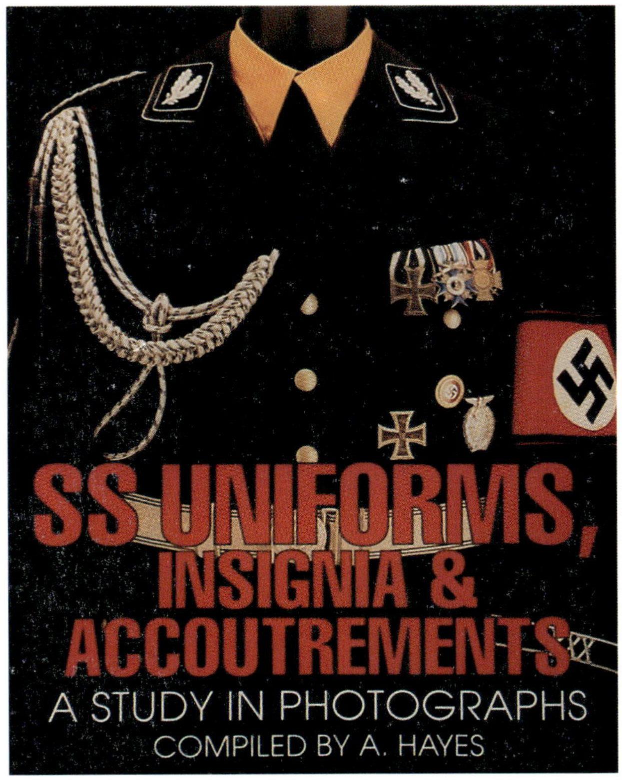

SS UNIFORMS, INSIGNIA & ACCOUTREMENTS

A STUDY IN PHOTOGRAPHS

Compiled by A. Hayes

Size: 8 1/2" x 11" over 800 color and b/w photographs
248 pages, hard cover
ISBN: 0-7643-0046-6 $69.95

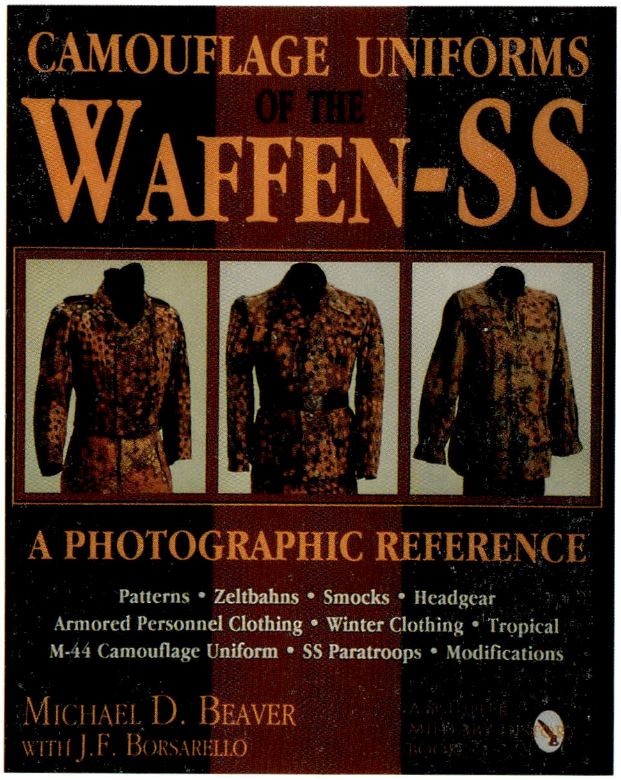
CAMOUFLAGE UNIFORMS
OF THE
WAFFEN-SS
A PHOTOGRAPHIC REFERENCE
Patterns • Zeltbahns • Smocks • Headgear
Armored Personnel Clothing • Winter Clothing • Tropical
M-44 Camouflage Uniform • SS Paratroops • Modifications
MICHAEL D. BEAVER
WITH J.F. BORSARELLO

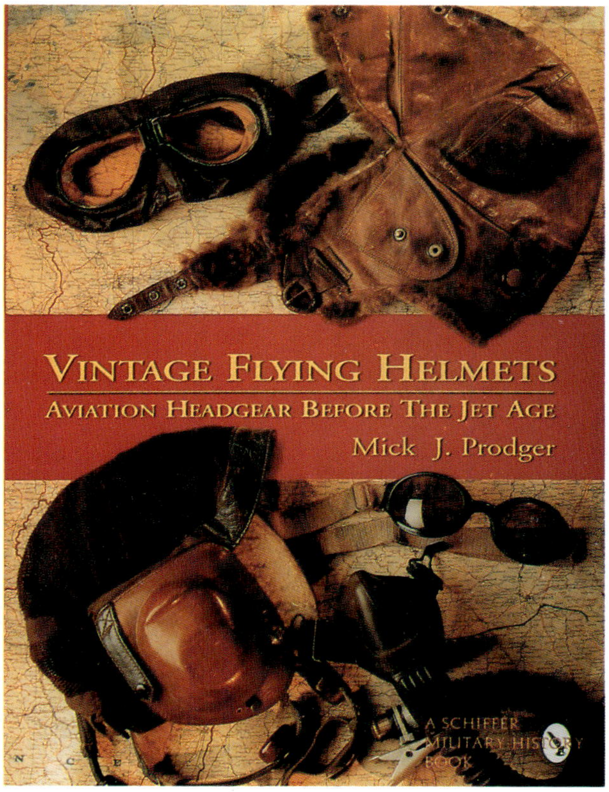

VINTAGE FLYING HELMETS

AVIATION HEADGEAR BEFORE THE JET AGE

Mick Prodger

Size: 9" x 12" over 1000 color and b/w photographs
336 pages, hard cover
ISBN: 0-88740-776-5 $75.00